IGBO ENTREPRENEURSHIP MODEL

A BUSINESS MODEL FOR ENTREPRENEURS

EMMANUEL ELAKHE

Keywords: Entrepreneurship, Business model, Culture, Capitalism

CONTENTS

	Introduction	5
1	Overview of Business Culture	9
2	Culture and Capitalism	15
3	Igbo Entrepreneurship Culture	20
4	Impact of Igbo Entrepreneurship Culture	25
5	Stages of Igbo Entrepreneurship	34
6	Igbo Entrepreneurship and Business Strategies	39
7	Igbo Entrepreneurship Model	43
8	Igbo Entrepreneurship Model Forecast	60
9	New Entrepreneurship Model	67
10	The Economics of Igbo Entrepreneurship	69
	Conclusion	
	Glossary	

INTRODUCTION

The increasing rate of growth in global businesses can among other things be unarguably attributed to a culture of hard work, discipline, commitment, persistence and intelligent use of available resources and technology. Culture has been defined as a way of life but can also be expanded to mean the way things are done among a particular people, place, society or organization. It encompasses the beliefs, values and attitudes accepted in a particular hemisphere comprising a group of people. If these beliefs, values and attitudes are imbibed by members of a business organization then it is called a business culture or organizational culture. Culture unites people, members of society, businesses or organizations and makes it easier to achieve the set goals of the society or business organization. Culture impacts on varied aspects of human endeavour- it affects the way we think, our actions and choices as individuals, it affects our communication patterns, how we manage people, how we make decisions on consumption, sales, risk propensity etc. We see a unique culture of the Latin Americans that have induced remarkable business success and has produced internationally recognized brand like Petrobras, Pemex, America Movil, JBS etc. Therefore the culture of a place evident in the lifestyle of the dwellers may influence productivity to a reasonable extent.

We also see the case of the Hispanics with a culture of persistence, communal cooperation and a culture that embraces technology, just to mention a few. As Cesar (2014), puts it, "a popular Mexican saying 'no te rajes' meaning 'don't back down". This talks about the culture of persistence imbibed among the Mexicans. The Hispanics also network and connect, they call their family and relatives to build and develop business opportunities. They don't downplay the importance of technology in business, no wonder over 80% of users of social media in the United States are Hispanics. (Cesar, 2014)

China has in recent years been ascribed as a nation that is gradually becoming the world economic superpower. This acclaimed position given to the Chinese is not unconnected to the success recorded by their businesses globally. There is, therefore, a lot to be learnt as regards this great success. In efforts to better understand the success secret of the Chinese, many have traced this secret, to their cultural heritage. This explains why the famous Chinese book 'The Art of War' which reflects part of the cultural heritage of the Chinese is been studied in many prestigious business schools across the globe. Some of the lessons learnt, that apply to today's business strategy include; How to plan your business, how to overcome competitors, how to manage resources efficiently, how to minimize cost-efficiently, how to channel energy and resources judiciously etc. (Huipeng, 2019). We see another practical example of this business culture; the business success link among the young men in Thailand who spend many years undergoing a religious entrepreneurship in Buddhist Monasteries, they claim that it is good for the Spirit and soul and influenced their pace in business and economic activities. Today the nation of Thailand grows very fast and this can be attributed to young men who subject themselves to a culture of weeks of meditation in the Monasteries.

It is also important to note that why some cultural beliefs and values may influence business performance positively, we might also see the case of a negative causal link. Southern Italy is a practical example, where culture has negatively impacted their ability to succeed in business. Alampi Jr (2007) describes the traditional southern lifestyle as one of the causes of poverty in southern Italy. Hentsch (2018), also asserts that the Italian culture has been one characterized by lack of boldness and an attitude of risk avoidance and as such not a culture that will support any reasonable growth in business.

It is against this backdrop that we seek to unveil the Igbo entrepreneurship model which was derived from a culture of business, hard work, persistence, zest, entrepreneurship, etc. This entrepreneurship model is divided into three types; Igba odibo, imu ahia and imu oru. These shall be further discussed in other sections of this book.

1   Overview of Business Culture

Historically there has been a strong connection between morals, beliefs, attitudes and economic progress. Researchers and business experts are increasingly interested in the role of cultural values on business and organizational performance, what is now called organizational culture. We, therefore, see that most of the top businesses were built on the foundation of strong organisational culture. The rise of the philosophy of capitalism itself was rooted in a cultural phenomenon embedded in the subject matter of 'religion'. Max Weber's Protestant ethic and the Spirit of Capitalism adequately explore this relationship. The protestant belief and values are rooted in hard work, excellence and the need to live and work in a certain way to attain riches as the end product. They, therefore, accorded importance to instructional literacy and time management which helped them to succeed in business and accumulate more capital.
Cultural values vary globally and directly and indirectly impact individual progress, business performance and national development. For instance, among the Western nations, parents give attention to the culture of individualism, self-reliance and autonomy among their children. If these attributes are found in them, it paves a way of determining the pace of progress expected from the child in the future. Therefore, once these values are encouraged and imbibed by their children, they tend to make significant progress in various aspects of their endeavour - education, business, politics, sports, etc. (Harrison and Huntington, 2000).
In China, the role of cultural values in business dates to

Confucius. The Confucian system established a monarchy system based on family hierarchy. This system was a central component of the Chinese, Korean and Japanese culture and was said to be a setback to the growth of most businesses in the East. This cultural belief evolved until it gradually came to an end at the advent of the communist party in China (Harrison and Huntington, 2000). In the second half of the 20th century, there was no history to match the dramatic reversals in the fortune of the Asian economies (Harrison and Huntington, 2000). The long-established assumption that Asian cultures could not generate business and economic growth was dramatically shattered within this period by the emergence of the 4 Asian tigers. The region became the envy of the developing economies. They have also formed a major component of skilled immigrants in the United States and Canada. But to tap into their talents and capabilities in business a good understanding of their culture is inevitable (Huipeng, 2009).

A study conducted by Kun-His (2017), on the impact of traditional Chinese culture on business relationships, revealed some major cultural characteristics which include iren-qing (personal relationship), mianzi (reputation), chaxu-geju (different mode of association) and collectivism which impacts on customer relationship marketing. These cultural characteristics can improve relationships with customers and thus create more consumer preference for the firm (Kun-His, 2017). Below, we shall summarize some of the core cultural business values held by the Chinese, which have influenced their businesses positively

Confucianism: Confucianism forms a major part of Chinese cultural values. These values uphold ethics in business and the good of all rather than just an individual. Some of the tenets of Confucianism include; (i) trust- a trust is a form of a bond among the Chinese businessmen, this important virtue ensures that no room is given to opportunistic behaviour. (ii) Reciprocity: business transactions thrive only on the substance of mutual benefit so that no one gets cheated. This sustains the business network and existing relationships. This relationship connection is referred to as *Guanxi* while the idea of exchanging benefits or reciprocating benefit is referred to as *renqing or simply exchanging favours*. *Renqing* is also a form of social currency in the sense that if you have accumulated enough personal favours you are said to have a strong *renqing* which can be used to initiate future transactions. The *renqing* cultural value has been used to sustain a business relationship between buyers and sellers, business partners for a very long period. This cultural values *cum* management approach has also been adopted by the Japanese and have been copied from the Japanese by many big firms globally (Harrison and Huntington, 2000). Other close ally nations have also had similar business cultural values which include; collectivism, the hierarchy management approach, time management, use of business cards, meeting management etc. These business norms have enabled them to grow their businesses and economy to such an extent that they became some of the strongest economies in the world (Gaw, 2016).

In Latin America, we have also had top businesses that have been a result of the practice of an existing culture. The core cultural values upheld by the Latinos which have enhanced their business strategy and performance include the culture of trust, building and maintaining good relationships, using technology in almost everything, risk-taking, high level of independence, persistence etc. These cultural values have enabled them to build global brands out of their businesses in the United States. (Loretta, 2010)

2   Culture and Capitalism

There is also a strong relationship between culture and capitalism. Certain aspects of culture and society can be said to be a product of capitalism. The culture of capitalism encourages people to engage in an activity that is deemed valuable by others. This is one of the most positive attributes of capitalism embraced by many (Price, 2005). Max Weber describes capitalism as a definite mode of life that shapes our relationships with others and our actions in the material world (Ferrarese and Cole, 2018).

This definition is strongly related to the concept of culture- which is the way of life, customs, beliefs, values, and the behaviour of a particular people or society. Marx attempts to approach the concept of capitalism from a holistic point of view devoid of prior perception, theory or belief that emphasizes the weaknesses of capitalism. The research proposes a new heuristic to comprehend capitalism broadly and deeply, it thus enables scholars to incorporate the diverse aspects of life in this new approach. Therefore, capitalism is seen beyond just a mere approach to acquire material wealth but also as a 'form of life' that presumes that all facets of life are inherently interwoven (Ferrarese and Cole, 2018).

The material prosperity in most of the Western nations especially America is rooted in a strong cultural foundation. The unique combination of cultural factors encouraged the emergence of capitalism (Miller, 2020). The average American culture is a culture that embraced self-sufficiency even before the advent of capitalism. Most individuals desired to provide their own needs with limited dependence on others and independent of the market system at that time (Price, 2005). The protestant ethics and the spirit of capitalism convincingly illustrate the important connections between culture and the economy (Nicki, 2019). Culture is a very important aspect of human endeavour which directly influences the economy. A study showed that cultural beliefs enhance people's trust (Guiso, et al, 2006). And it was demonstrated empirically that the level of trust (which can be derived from a strong cultural foundation) that people have in their country's institutions and fellow citizen influences many aspects of economic activity such as international trade (Olivier, 2019).

Protestant ethics is also another cultural belief that is strongly related to work and success at work. Protestant work ethic is the belief that work leads to success. This belief has pervaded many cultures across the globe and has been used to justify the reason for poverty in many nations (Bernardo, et al, 2018). The rising middle-class businessmen did not only show their wealth discreetly but also showed their proudly rigid self-discipline and thrift as a justification for the wealth they acquired (Goodrich, 2020). The protestant work ethic is meaningful in cultures that emphasize high individualism and personal responsibility. Countries with high individualistic cultures such as the United States have a strong relationship between work as a justification for success much more than countries with low individualistic cultures such as the Philippines (Bernardo, et al, 2018). There is a marked different orientation to work and leisure in some American and European countries like – the United States, United Kingdom, Japan etc. as compared to other American and European countries. The citizens of these countries are frantically known for their workaholic attribute and they see it as part of nature and common sense (Goodrich, 2020).

But where was this culture of hard work derived from? John Calvin taught many Protestants that ascetic dedication to one's perceived duties is "the means, not of purchasing salvation, but of getting rid of the fear of damnation. One must prove his faith by his worldly (economic) activity" (Goodrich, 2020). The Calvinists Protestants, therefore, viewed work as an important means of serving God. The culture was built on merit and hard work which helped them succeed in business (Says, 2010). Lutherans taught that paying careful attention to one's secular (economic) activities is humble obedience to God's will (Goodrich, 2020). So everyone did his work efficiently as a way of obedience to God's will. Benjamin Franklin, one of the founding fathers of the United States was neither a protestant Calvinist nor a Lutheran but adopted these principles from his father who was a Calvinist (Goodrich, 2020). Therefore Calvinism and Lutheranism gave birth to protestant work ethics and protestant work ethics gave birth to the spirit of capitalism in the United States and the United Kingdom. Capitalism was further adopted by other countries like China, Japan etc. (Zitelmann, 2019).

3 Igbo Entrepreneurship Culture

The Igbos occupy the South East of Nigeria, a territory which lies between latitudes 5 and 7 degrees north and latitudes 6 and 8 degrees east of the Greenwich line (Senan and Okwu, 2010). The Igbo culture has evolved from a decentralized leadership style in which control and allocation of resources are left in the hands of entities like kinsmen, age grade, and village groups etc. The Igbos practice a highly democratic system. The Igbo trade dates back as far as the Igbo culture. In 1823 John Adams identified the Igbo trading activities in the northern part of Nigeria among the Nupe tribe. The Igbos also had direct trade with the Europeans as early as 1870. Some researchers have acclaimed that this early trading relationship with the Europeans gave birth to the entrepreneurial prowess among the Igbos (Olutayo 1999; Onyeama1982). Nevertheless, they forget that other regions such as the Nupe in Northern Nigeria also had the same trade relationship with the Europeans and cannot boast of such exceptional skill. What was unique about the economic relations between the Igbos and Europeans was that they were intensive, continuous and of long duration which enabled them to acquire wealth, value and prestige (Olutayo, 1999).

The Igbos have a unique cultural value orientation that has arguably produced a unique business model and enabled them to expand their businesses easily. The communal civic spirit is one of the cultural values of the Igbos that enable them to thrive even outside their land. Some see this value as one of the lifeblood of the entrepreneurial ability of the Igbos globally. For instance the 'Igba mbo' or 'Igba boyi' cultural belief which means 'self-help' or 'self-enterprise' relates to the enterprising nature of the Igbo culture. Parents in the Igbo tribe start early enough to identify their children's entrepreneurial ability and ambition and then provide capacity building through a mentor-mentee relationship or a master-servant relationship. Through this process, the mentee or servant is allowed to start his own business after successfully undergoing apprentice training. The process goes through the following three stages; talent identification stage, learning stage, and final settlement or start stage (Iwara et al, 2019).

The kinship, brotherhood and cultural groups philosophy is also a major component of the Igbo culture usually referred to as 'Umunna Igwebuike" and 'Nwanne di na mba' meaning unity and strength together. This cultural practice has enabled most Igbo businesses to grow even outside their locality. The Igbo land is always not neglected, such that as Igbos grow their businesses outside the Igbo land they still have a coming back home mentality to grow a business and develop the community, this act is also enshrined in the Igbo culture.

Akpoyomare et al, (2013), identified some indigenous Igbo business and management practices in their study of the Igbo indigenous management concepts and practices. Nji ko ka; an indigenous Igbo concept which means resolving the agreement of all, this practice is an example of the democratic nature of the Igbo culture and enables a decision to be made easily without many disagreements and unnecessary grudges. 'Onye aghala nwanneya' is another concept which implies a form of the mutual exchange or mutual benefit or been your brother's keeper and can be compared to the Chinese Confucianism practice. This practice, like the Chinese businessmen, enables the Igbos to succeed together in trade without any been left behind. 'Igwe buike', which means unity in strength' achieves a similar goal with 'Onye aghala nwanneya'.-This practice enables the Igbos to unite in their business transactions. A united network ensures that when a buyer needs a product, one supplier in one location can reach another Igbo supplier in another location, transactions are made easy with little or no additional transaction costs. Such kind of network sustains the business relationship between them for a long period.

Obunike (2016), a study of the induction strategy of Igbo entrepreneurs and their success in micro-business identified *Igba odibo* as a unique apprentice strategy that has immensely contributed to business success and expansion across the Igbo land and beyond. It is an informal business school that brings the master (owner of the business) and the 'nwaboy' (learner) into close contact to transfer knowledge and experience from the master to the servant after which the servant is settled and becomes a master of his own. The study further identified other important types of entrepreneurship embedded in the Igbo business culture such as *imu-ahia*; this is a practice of coaching an individual who has the financial means but lacks the requisite knowledge and experience in a line of business he or she desires. Through the *imu-ahia* philosophy, the apprentice seeks a business coach and he or she is trained in that line of business. We also have the *imu-oru*; which involves learning the crafts of another vocation to enhance your skills. The graduates in Nigeria seeking white-collar jobs can adopt this practice to enhance their marketability in the labour market. The *'Igba-Oso-ahia"* is another Igbo business culture or strategy used to raise more capital by collecting a commodity at its given price and seeking ways to sell it at a higher price to earn more money and raise capital to start up your own.

4 Impact of the Igbo Entrepreneurship

Aba is one of the biggest commercial hubs in Nigeria and has been known globally for its expertise in shoe production- It has a shoe business valued at over 368 million dollars with a production capacity of about 4 million shoes per month (Business Day, 2019). Their leather works attract customers in West Africa, South Africa, China, Canada, and Europe etc. The shoe trade employs thousands with many learning and working as an apprentice as they specialize in different areas such as cutting, designing, stitching, skinning, peeling etc. As a commercial hub in Nigeria, their adept skills and dexterity can also be felt in other areas such as fashion, clothing, automobiles etc. they are sometimes referred to as the Japan of Africa.

There are 5 major markets in Aba with their various specializations; Ariaria market, new market, Ekeoha market, Cementry market and Alaoji market. Ariaria market known for shoe production had an annual turnover of about $3 billion and about 2 million traders in 2018 (*Chijioke, 2019*). The Newmarket is known for the sales of food items and second-grade clothing's. Ekeoha market harbours the largest fashion and clothing market in Nigeria, the market runs millions of transactions in textile monthly. While the Cemetery market is a market for products such as deodorants wine and food items and Alaoji market is a market for car spare parts.

Anambra state is widely known for its large scale trade and commercial activities in two of its major cities- Nnewi and Onitsha (Nevin and Olatunji, 2017). Nnewi is majorly known for its expertise in sales of car parts and assembling and manufacturing of cars and motorcycles. Nnewi city accounts for about 70% of auto parts (including motorcycle) and manufacturing business in Nigeria and serves as a major assembling hub for international auto companies (Nevin and Olatunji, 2017). Due to the enormous economic and business activities in Nnewi town, it has also attracted investment in financial institutions, which are majorly microfinance banks to cater for the needs of small scale enterprises and commercial banks to cater for the financial needs of medium and large scale businesses. Most of the markets in Nnewi harbours traders who specialize in different areas such as car parts, motorcycle parts, pharmaceuticals, building materials, textiles, stationeries, cosmetics, electric cables, food products such as palm oil, yam, cassava, cocoyam, breadfruit etc. They achieve these specializations through the practice of the Igbo entrepreneurship to train young ambitious learners who now become a master of their own. Nnewi is a self-sufficient economy that can survive and thrive with little or no government support through its large trading and farming activities. The farmers produce the food and sell them to the traders and industry workers, while the farmers also depend on the industries for their agricultural equipment and transport facilities.

Onitsha market is also in Anambra state. It has also been identified as one of the largest markets in West Africa. Onitsha market is so prominent that it is been studied in some Universities and forms part of their literature. Spencer research library at the University of Kansas (KU) for instance acknowledges and promotes the importance of Onitsha market literature in detailing what Chinua Achebe describes as " Social problems of a mixed-up and dynamic modernizing community" (KU Libraries, 2019).

There are several markets in Onitsha, numbering about 40 and are specialized in various trade. The major market is called the Onitsha main market, this market specializes in fashion, clothing and household items. Other major markets in Onitsha include; Relief market (dealers of canned drinks), Ose market (dealers of food items), Ochanya market (dealers of leather works and footwear), Electromart market (dealers of electrical appliances), Ogbo Ogwu market (dealers of pharmaceutical items), Ogbo Osisi market (timber dealers), and Ogbo Efere market (dealers in plastics, Aluminium, tires, cooking utensils etc.). Onitsha is the centre of commerce in Anambra state and can be referred to as the commercial capital of the state.

Onitsha market witnesses economic activities of about 2 million traders daily and creates about half a million jobs through the Igbo entrepreneurship (Mycostoma, 2017). A high inflow of goods and customers occurs in Onitsha daily. The annual turnover as a result of this trade is about 3billion dollars with over 12 million transactions from about 5 million buyers and sellers annually (Mycostoma, 2017).

The major trades in Onitsha include; Pharmaceuticals, cosmetics, clothing, banking (primarily microfinance banking to meet the financial capital needs of SMEs), plumbing materials, plastics, sachet or package water, polythene, textiles, shoe production, aluminium and welding, transportation, food and restaurant etc. The Onitsha business strategy is a strategy that co-opts almost all and sundry in the state into one economic activity or the other which has led to a reduction in the rate of unemployment and poverty in Anambra state. Almost everyone is saddled with one trading activity or the other, there is scarcely an idle charter or beggar. It is a typical example of a productive and working economy. If you don't own a business, trade or skill, you can learn and work under someone who owns one and those who do not fall under this category can offer direct labour haulage and earn a living (there is a great market for this in Onitsha because of the high volume of goods that are brought into the market daily).

Some Notable Businesses that were products of Igbo Entrepreneurship in Nigeria

Coscharis Group

Coscharis Group is a product of the Igbo entrepreneurship. It was established in 1977 by Cosmas Maduka, he started an entrepreneurship with his uncle at a very young age. During his years as an apprentice, he learnt how to trade in auto spare parts. After a while, he had to face the risk of having to start his own business at the age of 14 years, because his uncle asked him to leave, due to his newfound faith. He got settled with a seed capital of one dollar at that time in addition to the experience and skill he acquired in procurement and marketing of auto spare parts. After he left his uncle, he attempted partnership business twice but were later grounded due to irreconcilable differences. He then founded Coscharis group which has become one of the largest distributors of auto spare parts in Nigeria.

Orange Drugs

When you cannot afford a formal education, the Igbo entrepreneurship appears to be the most viable and affordable alternative. This was the story of Tony Ezenna who was forced to learn his father's trade when he could not afford formal education. His father owned a small chemist business, and from the experience and training, he acquired from his father's business he was able to set up a bigger one. With the requisite knowledge and experience, he translated a 36 dollars seed capital to a multibillion-dollar pharmaceutical business called the orange drugs.

Ibeto Group

Cletus Ibeto is another renowned entrepreneur, from Nnewi Anambra state Nigeria. He was groomed via the Igbo entrepreneurship. At the age of 13, when he just gained admission into secondary school, plans changed when his father decided to engage at least one of his children in informal education, rather than sending all of them to the formal education that his brothers were already attending at that time. Young Cletus found this very difficult to live with, after much resistance from the young boy, he later came to terms with reality. He started his newfound training and education, by working as an apprentice with his master for about 3 years and learning how to trade in auto spare parts.

Although the civil war almost shattered the learning process, he was able to raise venture capital from his brother and other sources to start up his own. He specialized in auto spare parts and monopolized the business at that time. As his investment grew in the sale of auto spare parts, he was then able to expand his business and became one of the largest spare part dealers in Nigeria as of 1995. He has now diversified into other sectors such as; petrochemical, Ibeto cement, hospitality industry, real estate, etc. He currently employs more than 5000 workers and is still counting.

Capital Oil

Ifeanyi Ubah's passion for trade led him to drop out of school to acquire his desired skills in the auto spare part business. This paid off as he was able to start up his own after his entrepreneurship training. He started dealing in the auto spare part business, gathered more experience in it and later diversified into tyre supplies and oil and gas. He was able to grow his business across Nigeria and Africa.

5 Stages of Igbo Entrepreneurship

Fig 1: Stages of Igbo Entrepreneurship

There are 3 stages in of Igbo entrepreneurship:

Stage I

This is the stage where you *find a master*. A master could be a person you are working for as an apprentice or nwaboy (igba odibo), a person you have paid to learn a particular type of trade (imu ahia) or a person you have paid to learn a particular type of craft (imu oru). You have to find a master in the trade or craft you desire to learn. In finding a master in the trade or craft, you have to make your intentions clear, define your goal of learning and possibly sign terms and agreement with the master stating what is expected of him and what is required of you at the end of the process.

Proximity is also an important factor you might need to take cognisance of, you have to find a master in a location not far from where you live, except your master accepts to accommodate you. It is at this stage agreements on how much you should pay (in the case of imu ahia and imu oru), how it should be paid and when it should be paid as agreed on to avoid future conflicts between the master and the learner in the course or after the learning process. For the igba odibo system, you have to also agree on whether there is going to be a financial settlement at the end of your service and learning process.

Stage II

Under stage two, you have found a master and must have started *learning the trade.* In this stage, it is expected of you to learn all the techniques in the trade or craft. This stage allows you to understand the business idea and strategy and ask all the questions you need to ask about the trade or craft. Stage II also exposes you to different types of skills such as marketing skills, procurement skills, risk management skills, customer relationship management skills etc. Your success or failure in the trade or craft is dependent on this stage. For instance, if you fail to catch the business idea and strategy, even if you are settled with a seed capital (for the igba odibo system) you may still likely fail in the business since you didn't understand it. Also if you don't behave well enough at this stage your master is not likely to settle you with a seed capital at the end of the training process. Therefore beyond understanding the business and acquiring the requisite skills, it is also a character-building stage. You must be humble and submissive to your master as you learn, you must be polite to customers, and you must be punctual to work.

This stage also lays the foundation for your startup, as you will have the opportunity to connect to prospective clients, suppliers, contractors etc. If you treat them well, they can support, patronize and connect you when you start your own business.

Stage III

At this stage you are expected to *start your trade* from the skill you have acquired, trade you have learnt and the venture capital you have been settled with. Your success or failure at this stage is dependent on your performance in stage II. You are completely responsible for your decisions, you are the sole owner, sole decision-maker and sole risk-taker. Stage I and II is the preparation and the learning stage. While stage III is the examination stage, if you prepared and learnt well in stages I and II, you are likely to be successful in stage III.

You are therefore expected to put all you have learnt together and begin to apply them in the field of business. In this stage you may meet giants like; setbacks, oppositions, unfavourable business environment, increasing costs, human limitations, limited resources, power failure, competitors, etc. All you have acquired in the learning stage (stage II) i.e. the management skills, soft skills, character-building skills will be of great help as you confront these giants.

6 Igbo Entrepreneurship and Business Strategies

The major types of business strategies are; cost leadership or cost differentiation strategy, product differentiation strategy, growth strategy, focus strategy etc. Below we shall consider how the Igbo business culture impacts business strategies.

I. Cost Leadership /Cost Differentiation Strategy

Cost leadership strategy relates to how firms can minimize the cost of production as compared to the cost incurred by other firms in purchasing the same quantity and quality of inputs. This will enable such firms to produce at a lower cost and sell at a cheaper price and higher volume. The Igbo entrepreneurship which grooms individuals in a particular trade, enables them to create a kind of network or informal association, such that they can buy these inputs in bulk at a lower cost. For instance, the apprentice who becomes a master is acquainted with almost all the information needed in a trade; including contacts of suppliers of inputs, contacts of those in a similar trade etc. and he can tap from such existing relationship when he starts his own to buy input at the same cost or a cheaper rate from the supplier like his master does. In some cases, the apprentice turned master can collaborate with his former master or those in similar trade to buy inputs on a larger scale and at a lower cost. In addition, Igbos in the same trade tend to network from their various locations and when they buy inputs they do it collectively and buy very large quantity bringing down the average cost per input and ensuring that they can produce the same product or output at lower cost and sell at a lower price as compared to their competitors. A practical example of a market where the cost leadership strategy is been practised by the Igbos is fashion design and shoe production in Ariaria market Aba and Motor spare parts across many markets in Nigeria.

In Aba, we see a high influx of individuals across Nigeria patronizing the fashion designers and shoemakers because of the quality of their products available at a lower price. The same quality of shirt that can be bought from online platforms like Jumia or any other supermarket at about 62.5 US dollars or more can be bought in Aba for about 37.5 US dollars. The same quality of shoe that might cost about 37.5 US dollars in Jumia, eBay, Konga etc. at can be obtained in Aba for about 20 US dollars. We see a lot of individuals take advantage of this price differentiation by buying in bulk to resell at a higher price in other parts of the country.

II. Product Differentiation and Focused Strategy:

Product differentiation and focused strategy is a strategy that enables producers to focus on the production of a unique product to carve a niche for themselves in the market on the production of that product. The Igbo entrepreneurship enables you to specialize in a certain type of trade or craft. This is why only the Igbos majorly specialize in certain types of trades in Nigeria like; shoemaking, sale of auto spare parts, computer repairs and accessories, motorcycle production and assembling, automobile production and assembling, fashion design, aluminium, fabrication, pharmaceuticals, etc.

III. Growth Strategy

The growth strategy is a strategy aimed at business expansion, the Igbo entrepreneurship is a perfect strategy for achieving business growth. An efficient apprentice will support the business of his master in such an effective way, such that as the business receives more clients he can be told to manage another branch with little or no supervision. In some cases, after the nwaboy completes his training instead of settlement, his master can open another branch for him to manage.

7 The Igbo Entrepreneurship Model

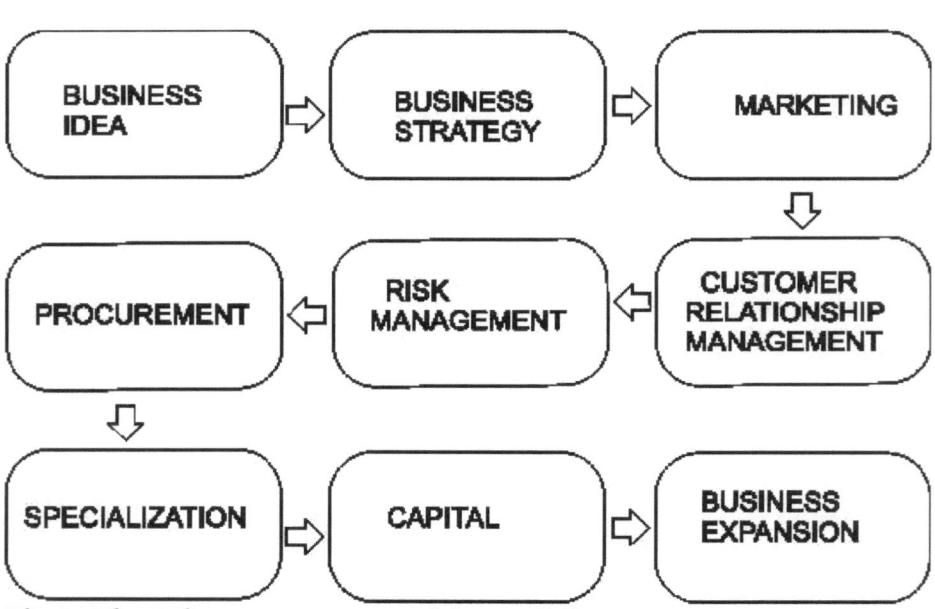

Fig 2: The Igbo entrepreneurship model

Business Idea

The business idea is the unique proposition of the business in which it is identified. A good understanding of the problem been solved, solution been created or value been added by the business concern is an important start point for the learner in the learning process. The concept of the business is the first thing the learner must catch after which others can be understood. An understanding of the business idea lays the foundation of the entrepreneurship. This can be caught either through direct transfer of knowledge from the master to the learner or through keen observation of the master by the learner. The learner can observe the day to day operation of the business, ask relevant questions, take note of details and even make more researches, this will enable him to understand the business idea better.

Business strategy

A good understanding of the business goals and how the business owner/master intends to achieve these goals is also important. A business strategy has to do with setting specific business goals and stating explicitly how such goals can be achieved. Most thriving businesses set goals - these goals must be specific, measurable, achievable, reliable and timely.

A good business strategy will keep the business relevant in the industry. As an apprentice or learner in the trade or craft, you are most times included in the business plan. For instance, the business owner might have a plan to expand his business by opening another branch after a year, he would therefore need the apprentice to manage the newly opened branch.

A good business strategy covers the present and the future, it defines the dos and the don'ts in the business. The type of trade or craft that is been learnt will determine the type of business strategy that will be the best fit. For instance, in the automobile spare part trade which is popular among the Igbos, the most viable strategy to be adopted will be either the cost strategy or the focus on a niche strategy. Businesses dealing in such trade will seek ways to procure spare parts at the lowest cost possible to maximize sales and revenue. They could also adopt the focus niche strategy, to have a speciality in one type of car parts since there are so many car parts and their prices are quite exorbitant, it will be best to focus on either a car part that is most popular in the market (e.g. Toyota) or a particular car part that is not popularly in demand but scarce in the market - In this case, you are sure that the few persons who will require such parts will always be directed to you since you are the sole seller of such parts.

A business strategy is always geared towards growth and expansion. The attainment of this goal depends on how efficient this strategy is and how well the roadmap has been adhered to. You cannot succeed as an entrepreneur, businessman or craftsman without a defined strategy. Therefore it is very important that the learner learns and develop his business strategy in the course of the entrepreneurship process.

Marketing

At this stage, you begin to understand how to act on your set goals to achieve them. Every product or service has a target consumer, the first step to marketing your product is to ascertain who needs the product. When that is established, you also have to know how much of such a product is needed i.e. what is the market for your goods and services. Is it a small market or a large market? And if the product is already in the market, how can I carve a niche for myself by making my product different and unique. Every product or service has its unique selling point. Since the idea has been developed into a product already, the learner must observe closely how his master uses the unique selling point of the product or service to attract customers to the business. It is not enough to have a product, achieving sales targets is also very vital. The learner can further research how the products can be sold. The marketing process also involves how to communicate these products to prospective buyers, how to negotiate to sell at a good price and how these goods are going to be delivered to the buyers. The emergence of internet technology has made marketing easier (We shall consider this in the reviewed model). Nonetheless, when the Igbo entrepreneurship system was introduced, technology was not predominant and because of the scarcity of some of these goods like the motor spare parts, not much marketing was needed for sales to be achieved.

Customer Relationship

You act on set goals by understanding how to manage customers efficiently. To run a business, among other things implies that you understand what it takes to keep the customers flowing in.

There is no business without customers and that's why the adage goes 'customer is always right. As an apprentice, you might have the opportunity to attend to customers, particularly when your master is absent. This is an opportunity for you to develop your customer relationship skills, you must treat the customers well and build a good relationship with them. How you treat them will determine the success of your business in the future, because they could be in a position to refer others to your business or give you contracts. We have the story of Sam Chukwunulonum, a major distributor of Hero Lagar beer, who was once an apprentice. His duty as an apprentice was to cross-check the invoice and identify mistakes. While doing that he was able to build a good relationship with the customers by helping them carry their loads to their cars even though that was not his responsibility. When he then started his own, it was easy for him to attract customers to his business based on the existing relationship he already had.

Part of building a good customer relationship involves; selling quality goods, keeping to your promise, attending to their request promptly, speaking to them politely, giving room for reviews, listening to their worries about a particular product or service, ensuring that they are satisfied with your goods and services, going beyond or raising the bar (if others can offer what you offer, then you must raise the bar to attract more customers), appreciating their patronage, reward their loyalty, make them establish trust with your business etc. Today we have technologies like the customer relationship management portal that enables you to manage your customers efficiently. This portal enables you to manage your company's relationship with customers and potential ones. It is also a platform for marketing your products, connecting with your customers, getting their feedback, etc.

Risk Management:

You need to understand how to manage the risk that arises as a result of achieving your business goals. There is no business without risk. Anyone who ventures into learning a particular trade or craft must also know the risk involved in it. A good knowledge of the risks involved and how to manage them lays the foundation for a successful business endeavour. The entrepreneurship model exposes you to risk because after learning the trade you are saddled with the task of starting up your own which comes with great uncertainties. Risks are uncertainties in the form of high costs, accidents, natural disasters, foreign exchange fluctuations, unfavourable weather conditions, financial errors, human failures, unfavourable government policies, procurement errors, competition, new technologies, legal risks etc.

Risks can be managed, and managing them begins with identifying them. You must identify as much as possible all the risks involved in a trade before you commence. The next step is to develop a plan on how to mitigate these risks. After proper analysis of the risks, you can then execute your plans.

Procurement

The business needs a trusted supply chain for unfettered supply of needed inputs. Procurement is a special skill that most learners acquire in the course of the Igbo entrepreneurship, if you learn under a motor spare part dealer, you must learn or acquire this skill to succeed in the trade. Procurement involves all the processes involved in purchasing goods and services for business purposes. Several steps must be taken for the successful procurement of goods and services. Firstly, you have to identify the goods and services that are needed by the business both in the current period and in the future (the future is considered because the prices of such goods might go up and become scarce if not bought in the current period). Secondly, you identify the list of available suppliers and contractors of such goods and services, you can research their offers or make contact with them. Thirdly, from the selected suppliers with offers that fit your demand, you can now negotiate terms with them. Fourthly, you finalize the purchase order, they process your invoice and you make payments so that your order can be delivered. Finally, as a skilled procurement officer do not forget to audit your goods when they are delivered, ensure that what was delivered corresponds to what was agreed in the contract terms. You should also assess the quality and return goods that are below quality. This must be done immediately after delivery is made so that goods can be easily returned without unnecessary delay and denial.

For instance, in handling a procurement process for motor spare parts, the following questions must be answered; what type of motor spare parts do I need? Where can I get the type of motor spare parts that I need? Are there available suppliers close to my location? Are there other competing suppliers with better offers? How can I negotiate their contract terms? How will these spare parts be delivered to me or how do I transport them? Where do I store these motor spare parts when they are delivered? How can I ascertain the quality of the spare parts delivered? The skills the learner needs to develop to be able to perform a successful procurement are; good communication skills, good negotiation skills, time management skills, critical and strategic thinking skills, financial management skills, etc.

Specialization:

Specialization occurs when you do a particular task over and over again. One major advantage the Igbo entrepreneurship has is that it enables you to specialize in an area of trade or craft over time. The first stage of the entrepreneurship is to find a master. In this sense you are to find one who is already a master in a particular trade or craft, you learn from that person and also become a master in that trade or craft. And the cycle goes on and on, it is therefore a model that produces specialities in a particular trade or craft. The model translates learners or apprentices' to masters.

You can specialize in a trade or craft when you focus on how to produce or sell a particular product or a limited number of products. There are different stages in a production process, you can therefore decide to specialize in a particular stage of production. For instance, in the production of automobiles, we have different stages in which different individuals may specialize to make the process more efficient. We have the design stage, construction, validation, quality assurance, assembling, sales etc. An apprentice can decide to learn a particular stage and specialize in it.

When you visit the Aba market in Abia state Nigeria, where automobile parts like; engines, gearbox, tyres, etc. are sold, you will discover that each dealer, deals in a particular area. We have those who sell a particular brand of a car engine, we have those who deal in gearboxes, we also have those who assemble them, we also have the mechanics who repair etc. Those who come to learn under them, choose an area in which they are interested in to learn and master over time.

Capital

Capital is the ultimate goal of the Igbo entrepreneurship model. The capital acquired at the end of the entrepreneurship process could be in the following form:

(i) **Human capital**: The skills, capabilities, abilities, potentials, etc. the learner acquires at the end of the entrepreneurship program is what we refer to as human capital. The entrepreneurship takes a period and within this period it is expected that the learner would have acquired and developed some skills, potentials, capabilities etc. which will enable him to succeed in running his trade. Human capital encompasses but is not limited to; training acquired, talents developed, knowledge acquired, creativity developed, experience, skills, etc.

(ii) **Social Capital**: This is another form of capital the apprentice is entitled to in the course of the learning process. This capital is acquired in the course of relating with customers, clients, suppliers, contractors, business partners, etc. They include all the relationships and networks you have built throughout your entrepreneurship and the positive impact they could have in starting up your own business. It may also include the associations you are privileged to be part of, the access to information from such associations, international networks and contacts etc.

(iii) **Physical Capital**: The learner may also be able to access physical capital. Physical capital is in the form of tools, machines, technology, buildings etc. that aids production. In some cases after learning a craft or trade your master may decide to spare some of his tools (those he has in excess) to enable you to start your craft, he may also give you a shop for free for a given period. Cosmas Maduka one of our case studies was able to get a shop for 6 months (although not from his master) without paying. By the virtue of the fact that you have learnt the trade or craft, individuals and businesses may be willing to assist you with physical capital to enable you to start up like it was in the case of Cosmas Maduka.

(iv) **Financial Capital**: This is the capital you are settled with in the form of cash or non-cash, to finance your business at the start-up stage. This type of capital applies to the igba odibo entrepreneurship model where the learner is both expected to learn and serve. At the end of this process, he is settled with financial capital for his service to start up his own. The financial capital could be in the form of grants, soft loans, profits, partnerships, etc.

Business Expansion:

Business expansion is usually part of a business strategy- which defines a plan on how to achieve a particular goal of expansion, increase in revenue, sales, etc. The purpose of the Igbo entrepreneurship model is for business expansion, and it can occur in two ways; when you learn a trade or craft from someone to start your own you have expanded the trading activities in that particular trade. Secondly under the igba odibo model where you are expected to serve and learn; your master can saddle you with the responsibility of running a branch of his business if he considers you suitable to do so.

The business expansion could also take the form of opening an existing product in another location (local and foreign), introducing a new product in the same industry, giving out the franchise of your business, acquisition, merger, etc. There are several ways to achieve a business expansion goal; first, you have to incorporate it in your business strategy, seek opportunities in new markets, recruit and train staff, merge or partner with other businesses, take advantage of acquisition opportunities etc.

8 Igbo Entrepreneurship Model Forecast

EMPLOYMENT FORECAST

Premise
- Ariaria market Abia state, Nigeria had a total of 31900 established businesses in 2019 (Chijioke, 2019)
- Innoson motors trains and settles at least 10 entrepreneurs every year (Innocent Chukwuma, 2021).

Assumptions
(i) Let's assume we have just one market and this market has 20000 established businesses (because not all markets may be as big as the Ariaria market with 31900 established businesses)
(ii) Each of the above markets in (i) trains and settles at least 3 entrepreneurs every year (not all businesses will have the capacity of Innoson motors to train and settle 10 entrepreneurs every year)

From the above premises and assumptions the following forecast can be derived for five years:

Table 1.1: **Employment Forecast**

Start-up Model	Assumption	Inputs	Year 1	Year 2	Year 3	Year 4	Year 5
No. Established Businesses	20000 established businesses	Training	80000 established businesses	260000 established businesses	800000 established businesses	1962000 established businesses	6822000 established businesses
No. of Entrepreneurs Trained and Settled in 1 year	3 entrepreneurs trained and settled per business in 1 year	Learning	60000 trained and settled entrepreneurs	180000 trained and settled entrepreneurs	540000 trained and settled entrepreneurs	1620000 trained and settled entrepreneurs	4860000 trained and settled entrepreneurs

From the above forecast, we noticed that;
- Increase in No. of established businesses = f(No. of entrepreneurs trained and settled each year)
- Also at the end of 5 years, we would have had a total of 6822000 established businesses and 4860000 trained and settled entrepreneurs.

NB: This is a forecast for just one market. Now imagine this model is adopted in all markets in a given country, the impact will be more tremendous.

OUTPUT FORECAST

Premise
80,000 shops in Aba Market, Nigeria produces 1 million pairs of shoe each week (Business Day, Jan 2019). Which means 52 million pairs of the shoe are produced in 52 weeks (one year)
The average price of a pair of shoes is $7 (Business Day, Jan 2019)
Output = Price * Quantity
Total output from the production of shoes in the Aba market in one year:
$7 * 52 million pairs of shoe = $364,000,000.00
Therefore the total output from the production of shoes from the Aba market in one year is equivalent to 364 million dollars

Assumptions
(i) Let's assume we have just Aba market, with each shop producing the same number of shoes per year. Therefore the average output of each shop owner in the production of shoes in one year is given as:
Total market output/No. of shops = $364 million/80 thousand shops
Total Annual Output per shop in shoe production = $4550
(ii) Each of the above markets in (i) trains and settles at least 3 entrepreneurs every year who also engages in the production of shoes. Let's assume they are able to produce shoes worth an output of $2500 each, per year (Since they are just entering into the market, they might not be able to produce as much as $4550)

From the above premises and assumptions the following forecast can be derived for five years:

Table 2: **Output Forecast**

Start-up Model	Assumption	Outputs	Year 1	Year 2	Year 3	Year 4	Year 5
Total output in the market per year	$364 million dollars output in the market	Total value of Pair of shoes	$964 million	$2.764 billion	$8.164 billion	$24.364 billion	$72.964 billion
No. of Entrepreneurs Trained and Settled in 1 year	3 entrepreneurs trained and settled by 80000 business in 1 year	Total No. of entrepreneurs	240,000 trained and settled entrepreneurs	720,000 trained and settled entrepreneurs	2,160,000 trained and settled entrepreneurs	6,480,000 trained and settled entrepreneurs	19,440,000 trained and settled entrepreneurs

From the above forecast, we noticed that;
- Increase in Output = f(No. of entrepreneurs trained and settled each year)
- Also at the end of 5 years, we would have had a total output of $72.964 billion and 19,440,000 trained and settled entrepreneurs.

NB: This is a forecast for just one market. Now imagine this model is adopted in all markets in a given country, the impact will be more tremendous.

9   The New Entrepreneurship Model

Fig 3: New Entrepreneurship model

Chioke (2019), in his new model, revealed how the existing entrepreneurship model can be reinvented and reviewed to fit into the impact of changes in technology on businesses. Young and ambitious entrepreneurs might not need to go through the entrepreneurship system for such a long time if they can leverage existing technology and information data to build their business faster. He exemplified his model by giving examples of three young Igbo entrepreneurs who are excelling in their business careers by exploring technology and leveraging data. These entrepreneurs include: Kingsley Ayogu (An Artist) - he is very skilled in the art of painting and explores the Instagram social medium to market his artworks, he started on a very small scale but has used this platform to reach many prospective clients globally, he currently earns $1000 per painting. Richard Odo, a fitness instructor uses the Facebook and Instagram social media platforms to market his skills and presently earns about 730 dollars per month. The last example is a former banker Chiamaka Obukwe who suddenly developed an interest in Tourism. She resigned from the bank to follow her passion and interest. She now goes on a personal tour and uses social media to advertise her tour after which she is contacted by individuals and organizations to organize trips on their behalf and she is paid heavily for her services.

According to Chioke (2019) by using existing technology and leveraging on existing data, the Igbo entrepreneurship model is reduced to a simpler model as shown in fig 5 above.

10 The Economics of Igbo Entrepreneurship

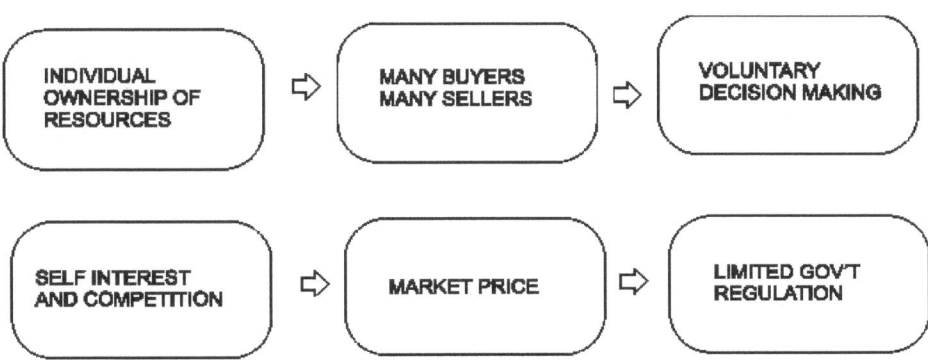

Fig 4: The market model

The Igbo Entrepreneurship is an example of a typical market economy. A market economy is one in which resources are owned and managed by individuals, decision making is also made voluntarily by these individual dealers in such a way that everyone aims to satisfy their self-interests of profit and utility maximization. There is also minimal government regulation nonetheless the economy is self-regulated by competing dealers (buyers and sellers) in the market. Some of the basic attributes of this market include:

(i) Individual Ownership of Resources

In a market economy, resources such as; land labour and capital are owned and managed by private individuals. Based on the Igbo entrepreneurship model, an individual who intends to start up a business such as, shoemaking, motor spare parts, etc. seeks one who is already a master in that trade or craft in order to be trained. When the training is completed, he acquires capital- which may be in the form of human capital, venture capital, social capital etc. He uses this capital to start up his own business. In order to achieve this, he needs to rent a space, buy capital goods, hire labour etc. And as his business expands, he may decide to train an apprentice who will also undergo the same process and the cycle continues. We, therefore, see a market where individuals enter freely, acquire capital, use the capital to create goods and services in order to own a share in the market. This results in a competitive market where all resources are owned and managed by private individuals seeking to maximize their various self-interests.

(ii) Many Buyers and Sellers

The Igbo entrepreneurship market is also a market of many buyers and sellers. All the markets where the entrepreneurship model have been applied are large markets where you have a reasonable number of buyers and sellers. For instance Ariaria market known for shoe, production has an average of about 2 million traders (Chioke, 2019).

(iii) Voluntary Decision Making

Decisions on what to produce, how to produce, what prices to charge etc. are determined by the activities of competing sellers and rational buyers in the market. The Alaba market in Lagos for instance is known for the sale of electronics. Transactions in this market are voluntary and each seller decides what to sell and how much to sell but may not sell at a price that is above the existing market price in order to maximize profit. The rational buyers also make a voluntary decision on what and who to buy from, but may not buy from a seller selling at a higher price above the existing market price.

(iv) Self-Interest and Competition

When dozens of electronic dealers in the Alaba market, Lagos act in such a way that each seller aims to sell in such a way as to maximize profit and each buyer aims to buy in such a way as to maximize satisfaction- they are all acting based on their own selfish interest. Nonetheless, the collective goal of production and consumption is in the process achieved. We therefore, see that self-interest is a motivator for economic activities in the Igbo entrepreneurship.

As more apprentices are been trained under the Igbo entrepreneurship. They enter into the market and create more competition since the market is structured in such a way that there are little or no barriers to entry. Competition regulates the activities of these self-interested participants in the market thereby putting a check to monopolistic tendencies, cheating, fraud, corruption etc. In the Aba leather market, for instance, we see a high level of competition among the shoe sellers. No single shoe seller is capable of influencing the market price. If you produce a lower quality shoe at a given price, the buyer will patronize another seller with better quality. Also if the price is too high, the customer will patronize those with lower prices. Therefore in order to remain in the market, a seller must produce quality shoes at affordable prices. No single seller can take advantage of self-interest to discriminate against any buyer since self-interest has been put under check by the competitive nature of the market.

(iv) Market Price

From our typical market in (iv) above. No single seller can influence the market price of electronics in the Alaba market. If a seller attempts to sell above the existing market price, such a seller may likely lose some customers and may not be able to maximize revenue and profit. As buyers will patronize other dealers. The buyers also seek to buy the same quantity and quality at a lower price in order to maximize satisfaction. These invisible forces of sellers and buyers in the market seeking to maximize their selfish interests is what determines the prices of electronics in the Alaba market.

(v)   Limited Government Regulation

The government intervenes in the market in the following way:
i. Infrastructure: The government intervenes in the form of providing infrastructure such as road, electricity, etc. for instance a road has been constructed in Ngwa road Aba where major trading

activities take place.

ii. Security: The government also provides security to some of these markets. In the Alaba market, Lagos the government complements the existing neighbourhood security to guard against breaking into people's shops.

iii. Ensuring law and order: In cases of crime, disruptions, corruption, etc. The government also intervenes through the security agencies to ensure law and order is restored to the market.

Conclusion

The crux of the Igbo business culture is their unique entrepreneurship model designed in such a way that everyone is given an opportunity. Ekekwe (2020), puts it this way; the Igbo entrepreneurship is not designed to have one Iroko tree but many trees in the forest. It is therefore a simple model that can effectively solve the problem of unemployment in Africa. It is also important to state that the successful Igbo entrepreneurship model was based on an understanding of the importance of hard work, trust, networks, relationships, individualism etc. in their business dealings. In essence, we can infer that among other factors the successful Igbo entrepreneurship was built on a bedrock of social capital.

It is important to state that there is no perfect system or model but one that can be subject to further improvement. It is in this light that I bring to the forefront the following recommendation(s):

1. **The Igbo Business School**

An establishment of an Igbo business school to formalize the Igbo business culture and strategy is a welcome idea. The Igbo business school will give room for prospective students and entrepreneurs to learn from established entrepreneurs, researchers, business experts etc. They will have the opportunity to learn both the theoretical and practical aspects of a business. This institution will generate research products that will be very relevant in policy formulation. The institution will also generate employment opportunities, attract investment in the South East region or wherever it is sited. Established businesses in the region will also be enhanced through the provision of professional consultancy services by the institution.

2. **Technology**

Although many in the region have adopted technology in their various businesses. But a good number of small and medium-sized businesses in Aba, Nnewi and Onitsha are yet to take full advantage of technology in enhancing their business. As stated earlier, if technology is fully adopted the business model is made simpler.

REFERENCES

Akpoyomare O.B, Chinyere A.G. and Lateef K.O. (2013). 'Indigenous Management Thoughts Concepts and Practices: The Case of Igbos of Nigeria. Australian Journal of Business and Management Research. Vol.3 No.01 [08-15] | April-2013, ISSN: 1839 – 0846

Allan Bernardo ,Sheri Levy and Ashley Lytle (2018) 'Culturally Relevant Meanings of the Protestant Work Ethic and Attitudes towards Poor Persons' accessed in October 25th 2020 Culturally Relevant Meanings of the Protestant Work Ethic and Attitudes towards Poor Persons - PubMed (nih.gov)

Alyson Cole and Estelle Ferrarese (2018). 'How Capitalism Forms our Lives' May 28 2018 Full article: How capitalism forms our lives (tandfonline.com)

Andrew Nevin and Gbenga Olatunji (2017). 'Promoting Economic Prosperity: Analysis of the State Level Business Environment in Nigeria' accessed in Promoting Economic Prosperity (pwc.com)

Babara Goodrich (2020). 'The Protestant/Calvinist Work Ethic'

Ballesteros, Valerie V., (2017) "The Impact of Culture on Hispanic Entrepreneurs as Mediated by Motivation, Challenge, and Success". *Theses & Dissertations*. 319. htps://athenaeum.uiw.edu/uiw_etds/319

Bhasin Hitesh (2019). '3 Main Types of Business Strategies' accessed in 3 Most Important Types of Business Strategies Business Need to Focus - Talentedge Learning Series

Brautigam Deborah (1997). 'Substituting for the State: Institutions and Industrial Development in Eastern Nigeria. World Development Vol. 25 No. 7 pp. 1063-1080 Elsevier Science Ltd

Bul-Godley Elish (2019). "The Art of War-A13 Point Plan to Mastering Businessm accesed in January 14 2013, The Art of War - a 13 point plan to Mastering Business Strategy (tweakyourbiz.com)

Chioke Ike (2019). Reinventing Enterprise n' Ala Igbo, accessed in March 5th, 2019 (205) NKATA UMU IBE | MARCH 2019 FULL VIDEO - YouTube

Cole, Nicki Lisa, Ph.D. "Max Weber's Key Contributions to Sociology." ThoughtCo, Aug. 28, 2020, thoughtco.com/max-weber-relevance-to-sociology-3026500 Sociology'

Emeka C.G. and Chukwudi E.E (2017). 'The Ontological Foundation of Igbo Entrepreneurship: An Analytical Investigation. Journal of Philosophy Culture and Religion. Vol 33. 2077 www.iste.org

Emeka Ginigaeme (2019). 'The Culture of Igba Odibo (Igbo Apprenticeship) in Igbo land, accessed in September 28 2019, Apprenticeship) In Igbo Land - Anaedo Online

Eregha Bright (2019). 'The Igbo Business Model: A Catalyst for SMEs Development in Nigeria', accessed in Spetember 6 2018, The Igbo Business Model: A Catalyst for SMEs Development in Nigeria. - Wanbaba Blog

Gao Hongzhi. (2017) Chinese business values: Guanxi, mianzi, renqing, accesed in 22 September 2017, Chinese business values: Guanxi, mianzi, renqing (asiamediacentre.org.nz)

Geoffrey Anyanwn et al (2019). 'Apprenticeship: Dying engine of Igbo business model' accessed in September 9, 2019 Apprenticeship: Dying engine of Igbo business model – The Sun Nigeria (sunnewsonline.com)

Guiso, Luigi, Paola Sapienza, and Luigi Zingales. 2006. "Does Culture Affect Economic Outcomes?" *Journal of Economic Perspectives*, 20 (2): 23-48.

Harrison Lawrence and Huntington Samuel (2000). 'Culture Matters: How Values Shape Human Progress

Hero Lager (2021). 'Documentary on Igbo Apprenticeship System', accessed in April 14th, 2021 (205) The Hero's Walk - Documentary on the Igbo Apprentice System - YouTube

Iler Huiping (2009). 'Share Understanding Chinese culture leads to business success', accessed 15 June 2009, Understanding Chinese culture leads to business success (Guest commentary) | Canadian HR Reporter

Innoson Group (2016). 'About Innoson Group' accesed in about us – Innoson Group of Companies

Iyatse Geoff (2020). 'Nnewi: Nigeria's Self-Made Industrial Hub'. Business news accessed in March 2020 Nnewi: Nigeria's self-made Industrial hubBusiness — The Guardian Nigeria News – Nigeria and World News

Juwon Johnson and Nafiu Akeem (2014). 'An Exploratory Study of Igbo Entrepreneurial Activity and Business Success in Nigeria as the Panacea for Economic Growth and Development. International Journal of Scientific and Technology Research

Jacques Olivier (2014). 'Culture and Economy: Understanding the Dynamics of Globalization' accessed in March 2014 Culture and the Economy: Understanding the Dynamics of Globalization | HEC Paris

Kun-Hsi Liao (2017) Impact of Traditional Chinese Culture on Business-to-Business Relationship Marketing and Service Firm Performance: Pages 277-291 Published online Download citation
https://doi.org/10.1080/1051712X.2016.1250594

M Says (2010). 'Pop culture and the Spirit of Capitalism' accessed in October 18, 2010 Pop Culture and the Spirit of Capitalism « Kristin Does Theory (umwblogs.org)

Michael Miller (2021). 'Does Capitalism Destroy Culture" accessed in February 10 2021 Does Capitalism Destroy Culture? -

Intercollegiate Studies Institute (isi.org)

Mycostoma (2017). 'About Onitsha Market' accessed in About Onitsha Market – MyCostoma

Nworah Uche (2011). 'Cultural and Igbo Business Practices'. Accessed in June 6th 2011 Culture and Igbo Business Practices | Sahara Reporters

Obunike C.L (2016). 'Induction Strategy of Igbo Entrepreneurs and Micro-Business Success: A Study of Household Equipment Line, Main Market Onitsha, Nigeria. Accessed in 28 December 2016, Induction Strategy of Igbo Entrepreneurs and Micro-Business Success: A Study of Household Equipment Line, Main Market Onitsha, Nigeria in: Acta Universitatis Sapientiae, Economics and Business Volume 4 Issue 1 (2016) (sciendo.com) https://doi.org/10.1515/auseb-2016-0003

Ofurum Godfrey (2020). 'FG to Establish Automobile Industrial Park in Nnewi', accessed in, Business Day Feb 22, 2020, FG to establish automotive industrial park in Nnewi - Businessday NG

Ojo Ebunoluwa (2019). 'Biography and Life History of the Founder of Coscharis Group' accessed in Cosmas Maduka - Biography And Life History Of Coscharis Group CEO (entrepreneurs.ng)

Okoli Anayo et al (2020). 'Apprenticeship: The secret of business successes in Igbo land' accessed in November 4, 2020 Apprenticeship: The secret of business successes in Igbo land (vanguardngr.com)

Olawoyin Oladeinde (2020). 'Despite Thriving Business Aba remains a Pigsty'. Premium Times Thursday May 21 2020, accessed in, Despite thriving businesses, Aba remains a pigsty | Premium Times Nigeria (premiumtimesng.com)

Olutayo Olanrewaju (1999). "The Igbo Entrepreneur in the Political Economy of Nigeria. African Study Monographs,20(3): 147-174, September 1999, accessed in (3) (PDF) The

Igbo Entrepreneur in the Political Economy of Nigeria (researchgate.net)

Onyeije Mirabel (2021). 'The Igbo Apprenticeship System: Successes and Lessons' accessed in February 16, 2021 The Igbo Apprenticeship System: Successes and Lessons - Terraskills

Redahlia (2021). 'Cletus Ibeto – Biography And Success Tale Of The Founder Of Ibeto Group' accessed in Cletus Ibeto - Biography And Success Tale Of The Founder Of Ibeto Group (entrepreneurs.ng)

R.G. Price (2005) Understanding Capitalism IV: Capitalism Culture and Society' accessed in February 4, 2005 Understanding Capitalism Part IV: Capitalism, Culture and Society (rationalrevolution.net)

Senan Augustine and Okwu Ogunyeremuba (2010). 'Igbo Culture and the Christian Missions' accessed in Igbo culture and the Christian missions, 1857-1957 : conversion in theory and practice in SearchWorks catalog (stanford.edu)

Startuptipsdaily (2020). 'How The Son of a Nigerian Micro-Scale Chemist Built A Multi-Million Dollar Business' accessed in December 27, 2020 Biography & Success Story Of Tony Ezenna: CEO Of Orange Drug Groups (startuptipsdaily.com)

Victor A.C. (2020). 'Entrepreneurial Mindset of Indigenous Igbo Entrepreneurs: Critical Success Factors: Critical Success Factors'. International Journal of Entrepreneurship Vol. 4 Issue 1 pp. 1-10, 2020

Wilcock Michael (2001). 'The Place of Social Capital in Understanding Social and Economic Outcome' accessed in 1824913.pdf (oecd.org)

Zetlin Minda (2013) How Latinos have changed US Business Culture, accessed in July 10, 2013, How Latinos Have Changed U.S. Business Culture | Inc.com

Zitelemann Rainer (2019). 'China's Economic Success Proves the Power of Capitalism' accessed in July 8 2019 China's Economic Success Proves the Power of Capitalism (forbes.com)

Acknowledgements

To Prof. Franklin Ngwu: Thanks for reviewing part of this work, when it was to be published as a research article.

To Walter Ngwu: Thanks for your support in making a reference available when I dearly needed it.

To Nasara Amos Victor (The Professional Artist): Thanks for all that you do to bless humanity with your God-given talent and for taking out time to design a beautiful book cover, thanks a million.

To my family members: Thanks to all of you for always rendering your moral support.

To my wife to be: Thank you for who you are and what God has ordained for us in the future.

To my Igbo brothers and sisters: Thanks for your resilient, industrious and innovative culture and for the great impact you all make in the business world.

To my clients and readers: Thanks for making this book worth writing, and for your feedback and encouragement. I hope you find this book resourceful and helpful in your business career and your other endeavours.

To God Almighty: The creator of heaven and earth, The one who was and is to come, The giver of knowledge, wisdom and insight, My Hero, My Redeemer, My Helper, My Saviour, My Director, and my All in All. I give you all the glory for making this book a great success.

About the Author

Emmanuel Elakhe is an entrepreneur, author, and writer. His writings are focused on Economics, Morality, and Culture. His research on The Role of Morality in Economic Development has attracted more than 8000 reads and seven citations. He is also the author of the thesis Fiscal and Monetary Policy and Economic Growth in Nigeria; A comparative analysis. Published with Grin Munich, Germany.

Emmanuel Elakhe was selected as one of Nigeria's University brightest graduates to be part of the Young talent program of the Lagos Business School in August 2017. He also won the Tony Elumelu entrepreneurship award in March 2018 and has been a member of the entrepreneurship organization.

He has a Master's Degree in Development Economics, a certificate from Project Management Professional in Project Management Entrepreneurship. And he is currently involved in the Nambuit Project as a Project Coordinator.

Glossary

Aku luo uno okwuo ebe osi: This means a call to take one's business and wealth home in the Igbo culture

Ariaria market: The name of a market in Aba where shoes and other leather products are sold

Alaoji Market: The name of a market in Abia state Nigeria

Chaxu-geju: Meaning different modes of association in the Chinese language

Ekeoha Market: The name of a market in Abia state Nigeria known for fashion and clothing

Cemetery Market: The name of a market in Abia state Nigeria

Eke Amaobi Market: The name of a market in Nnewi, Anambra state Nigeria

Eke Ochie Market: The name of a market in Nnewi, Anambra state Nigeria

Eke Idi Orie Otube Market: The name of a market in Nnewi, Anambra state Nigeria

Electromart Market: The name of a market in Onitsha, Anambra state Nigeria, known for the sale of electrical appliances

Guanxi: It simply means a relationship in the Chinese language

Igba-Odibo: This is a form of entrepreneurship in the Igbo culture that brings together the master (owner of the business) and the learner (usually called nwaboy) to impart knowledge and skills of the business from the master to the nwaboy.

Igba Mbo or Igba boyi: An Igbo culture terminology that means 'self-help' or 'self-enterprise'

Iren-quing: A Chinese terminology that implies a personal relationship

Imu ahia: A philosophy in the Igbo culture in which an apprentice seeks a business coach to get trained in a particular line of business.

Imu-oru aka: In Igbo culture, this means learning the craft of another profession to enhance your skills.

Igba-oso-ahia: An Igbo business strategy used to raise more capital by collecting a commodity at a given price and seeking ways to sell it at a higher price to raise capital to start up a new business.

Innoson: The name of the first Indigenous car manufacturing and assembling plant in Nigeria.
Ose Market: The name of a market in Onitsha, Anambra state Nigeria, known for the sale of food items
Mianzi: A Chinese terminology that could be called 'reputation'
Nwaboy: The name given to the learner in the Igbo entrepreneurship (Igba-odibo entrepreneurship)
Nwanne di na mba: This means unity in strength in Igbo language.
Nji ko ka: This means reaching a resolution through the agreement of all in the Igbo culture.
Nkata Umu Ibe: This is a monthly symposium organized by some Igbo professionals, where presentations are made on relevant topics that affect the Igbos
Naseni M1: The name of the first made in Nigeria motorcycle in Anambra state, Nigeria.
Nkwo Market: One of the largest markets in Anambra state, Nigeria known for sales of car parts.
Nwafor Market: The name of a market in Nnewi Anambra State, Nigeria.
Ochanya Market: The name of a market in Onitsha Anambra state, Nigeria, known for leather works and footwear
Ogbo Ogwu Market: The name of a market in Onitsha Anambra state, Nigeria known for the sale of pharmaceutical items
Ogbo Osis Market: The name of a market in Onitsha, Anambra state Nigeria, known for dealing in timber
Ogbo Efere Market: The name of a market in Onitsha, Anambra state Nigeria, known for the sale of plastics, Aluminium, tires and cooking materials
Onye aghala Nwanneya: This is a form of a mutual exchange or benefits in the Igbo culture
Renqing: A Chinese terminology that implies exchanging benefits
Umunna Igwebuike: This means a cultural group or brotherhood philosophy in Igbo

www.ingramcontent.com/pod-product-compliance
Lightning Source LLC
Chambersburg PA
CBHW040241220526
45473CB00001B/331